A Growing Flower

By Esther Goh

Illustrated by Jovan Carl Segura

Library For All Ltd.

Library For All is an Australian not for profit organisation with a mission to make knowledge accessible to all via an innovative digital library solution. Visit us at libraryforall.org

A Growing Flower

This edition published 2022

Published by Library For All Ltd
Email: info@libraryforall.org
URL: libraryforall.org

Library For All gratefully acknowledges the contributions of all who made previous editions of this book possible.

This book was made possible by the generous support of Save The Children.

Save the Children

Original illustrations by Jovan Carl Segura

A Growing Flower
Goh, Esther
ISBN: 978-1-922827-85-2
SKU02689

A Growing Flower

These are flower seeds.

Seeds need water.

Seeds need sunlight.

Seeds need air.

Where is the air?

As they grow, seedlings need to be placed in soil.

As the seedling grows, there will be leaves and a stem.

Can you point to where they are?

Roots will also grow.

With constant care,
a flower will grow.

Here is how flowers
grow again.

Can you tell me what flowers need to grow?

You can use these questions to talk about this book with your family, friends and teachers.

What did you learn from this book?

Describe this book in one word. Funny? Scary? Colourful? Interesting?

How did this book make you feel when you finished reading it?

What was your favourite part of this book?

download our reader app
getlibraryforall.org

About the contributors

Library For All works with authors and illustrators from around the world to develop diverse, relevant, high quality stories for young readers. Visit libraryforall.org for the latest news on writers' workshop events, submission guidelines and other creative opportunities.

Did you enjoy this book?

We have hundreds more expertly curated original stories to choose from.

We work in partnership with authors, educators, cultural advisors, governments and NGOs to bring the joy of reading to children everywhere.

Did you know?

We create global impact in these fields by embracing the United Nations Sustainable Development Goals.